THE MIDDLE SCHOOL SURVIVAL
HANDBOOK™

HOW NOT TO CHOKE ON TESTS

ACHIEVING ACADEMIC AND TESTING SUCCESS

STEPHANIE WATSON

rosen publishing's
rosen
central®

Published in 2013 by The Rosen Publishing Group, Inc.
29 East 21st Street, New York, NY 10010

Library of Congress Cataloging-in-Publication Data

Watson, Stephanie, 1969–
How not to choke on tests: achieving academic and testing success/Stephanie Watson.
    p. cm.—(The middle school survival handbook)
Includes bibliographical references and index.
ISBN 978-1-4488-8310-3 (library binding)—
ISBN 978-1-4488-8315-8 (pbk.)—
ISBN 978-1-4488-8316-5 (6-pack)
1. Test-taking skills—Handbooks, manuals, etc. 2. Academic achievement—Handbooks, manuals, etc. I. Title.
LB3060.57.W38 2013
371.26—dc23

2012009245

Manufactured in the United States of America

CPSIA Compliance Information: Batch #W13YA: For further information, contact Rosen Publishing, New York, New York, at 1-800-237-9932.

CONTENTS

INTRODUCTION

It's the day of the big test—the day you've been dreading since your teacher first announced the test. You've studied and studied, but you're still stressed out.

As you frantically watch your teacher hand out the test papers, your forehead breaks into a cold sweat. You feel dizzy and anxious. Your stomach is like a giant ball of knots.

Around you, everyone seems cool, calm, and collected. They pull out their pencils and start writing. Your own pencil is frozen. The page looks like a mess of squiggly letters. Nothing makes sense! Your mind is going blank. You're going to get an F.

That one F will drop your grade for the whole year. It will carry over to the rest of middle school and then to high school. You'll never get into a good college, and you'll never have a career.

When you're not prepared for a test, all of these panicky scenarios might run through your mind. You can get so stressed out that you choke. One out of every three students is so nervous before a big test that it affects his or her performance, according

Being unprepared for a test can lead to a lot of unnecessary anxiety. When you study, you won't be nervous and you'll be more likely to do well on the test.

to an article in the October 2011 *Wall Street Journal*. Why are tests the cause of so much fear and loathing among students?

Back in elementary school, tests weren't as much of a big deal. Homework, projects, and class participation were all parts of the final grade. The grade may not have even been a letter, but a number or an "S" for satisfactory.

In middle school, tests are more important. They count for a larger percentage of your grade. Teachers, parents, and peers can all pile pressure on you to get good grades. That pressure can build up and become overwhelming if you let it get to you.

Test taking doesn't have to be a stressful experience as long as you change the way you look at it. Remember this: tests aren't given to stump students or to make them panic. One bad test won't ruin your grade for the year, and it certainly won't keep you out of a good college or prevent you from having the career you want. Tests are just a way for teachers to find out how much of the material students have learned and what areas they still need to work on.

No matter what your ability or learning style, you can ace every test—if you follow a few simple strategies. The first is studying. When you study, you need to be motivated, be organized, and use smart techniques. The second strategy is to get help when you need it—asking your teachers, parents, and even your friends to go over material you don't know and to help you review. The third strategy is to conquer your anxiety, so you don't sweat every time a teacher hands you a test.

CHAPTER ONE

STUDY SAVVY

Tests aren't meant to make students regurgitate a bunch of information they've crammed into their brain onto a piece of paper. They're designed to find out how much students have learned. The key word here is "learned."

When you take a test, you should know the material so well that you can express it in your own words, analyze it, and criticize it. How do you make sure you know your stuff on test day? By studying for it ahead of time.

Studying isn't as easy as it sounds. In fact, it's work. It can be challenging to work with so many distractions—like your friends waiting to play outside or the cool new video game sitting in your den. Which would you rather do, study or play? A lot of students would say "play," which is why motivation needs to be at the top of your study savvy list.

Getting Motivated

You *hate* history. Hate it. However, your lack of interest in the subject isn't going to make next week's test go away. Though you may never learn to love history (or math, English, or science), you can find something about every subject that sparks your interest. Say you're learning about the Fifth Amendment. It's boring you to tears. Try looking at the subject in a different way. You could search for news articles about murderers or thieves who invoked their Fifth Amendment rights while on the stand during a court trial for their crimes. On the other hand, you might find that the amendment of the U.S. Constitution comes in handy when your mother asks whether you broke her vase ("I plead the fifth!," you can respond). Putting the topic into a real situation not only makes learning about it more fun but can also help you understand it better.

Taking Notes

Your brain—though surely brilliant—is not a supercomputer. Most people can't listen to a half-hour lecture and remember every word of it an hour later, much less on test day. That's why note taking is one of the biggest study allies.

The first part of taking notes is effective listening. You need to pay attention to the words that are coming out of your teacher's mouth, not thinking about what sandwich your mom packed for lunch or which friend you're inviting over after school. Good listening involves your ears and the rest of your body. Sit up straight. Make eye contact with your teacher. Participate by raising your hand when she or he asks a question. Are you listening? Good! Now you're ready to start taking notes.

To help organize your notes, write a title at the top of each page. That title should represent the main topic covered in class that day; for example, "Bloodiest Civil War Battles" or "The Love Lives of Protozoa."

Now, start writing. Don't write down every single word your teacher says, especially if she tends to veer off subject ("Speaking

When taking notes, stick to the main ideas. Use abbreviations to write more quickly. You can go back to fill in any gaps in your notes after class or at home.

of Abraham Lincoln, let me tell you about the black hat I bought yesterday…"). Just write the main ideas. Sometimes you can tell the main ideas because your teacher writes them on the chalk-board or SMART Board.

Use bullet points to make the main topics easier to find. During a lecture on the bloodiest Civil War battles, your notes might look like the following:

- Battle of Gettysburg. Fought from July 1 to 3, 1863, in Gettysburg, Pa.
    - o Confederate Gen. Robert E. Lee's army went up against Gen. George Meade's Union Army.

■ Fifty-one thousand soldiers died, wounded, or missing.
  • More than half were Confed. soldiers.
    o Union Army won battle.
  • Battle of Chickamauga. Fought Catoosa and Walker Counties, Georgia, Sept. 18–20, 1863. The Army of the Cumberland (Union) vs. Army of Tennessee (Confed.). More than 34,000 soldiers died. Confeds. won.

As you can see in this example, you can use abbreviations—your own sort of shorthand—to help you write faster. "Confederate" is "Confed.," "General" is "Gen.," and so on.

Write as clearly as possible. Your notes won't do you any good if you can't read them. To improve readability, highlight or underline important passages so you can easily find them later. After class, look up any words or ideas you don't understand or ask your teacher about them.

If you're a sloppy note taker, ask your teacher if you can type them on a computer or record them on a digital recorder. Recording also makes it easier to check back on a fact you didn't hear or understand during class.

Every day when you get home after school, reread your notes. Try to explain them in your own words, so you know that you understand them. Reviewing your notes every day will make it easier to study for the test.

Organizing Your Time and Thoughts

Can you see your desk at home or is it buried under a mound of old tests, books, notes from your friends, and pictures? Do you fold your clothes neatly when you take them off or throw them

Give yourself enough space at home to study. Clear your desk of any clutter, and make sure it's away from any distractions, such as the television or computer.

fold your clothes neatly when you take them off or throw them in a corner of your room? The clutter in your bedroom tells a lot about your organizational skills—and whether you need to work on them.

To help organize your time and space, every Monday after school, write in a calendar or planner all the assignments and tests that are due for the week. Plan out how much time you'll need each day to finish homework and study, and write the times on your calendar. For example, the Tuesday entry might be: thirty minutes history paper, twenty minutes math problems, twenty minutes studying for Spanish test. Check your planner every single day.

Clear your calendar during big test weeks. Skip your favorite TV show, put away the video games, and don't make plans with friends so you'll have more time to study.

Keep your backpack, desk, computer, and notebooks well organized. Use folders and dividers so you can find what you need—books, study sheets, or pencils—without having to search for them. Every couple of months, throw out old tests, papers, and other junk that's started to collect. Also clean out your desk at home so it doesn't get too messy. If you take notes on your computer, organize your folders. Label every document by topic and date, and put it in an appropriate file. These few seconds could save you hours of searching for documents.

Winning Study Techniques

Now you're organized and ready to go. It's time to start studying! First, though, you need a place where you can be alone. Studying in the living room while your sister is watching *Glee* is not a good idea. Distractions like the television, computer, video games, and cell phones make it harder to concentrate and remember. Go to a quiet room, whether that's a bedroom, an office, or the basement. Study at a desk, sitting up straight—not lying on the bed or floor.

To help you study more effectively, break study sessions into small chunks of time (called "chunking"). Instead of studying an entire hour for your history test, study for just fifteen minutes every day for four days. That sounds much more manageable, doesn't it? You'll be amazed at how quickly the study time flies when you break it up.

Write a question on one side of each note card and the answer on the other side. Use the cards to test yourself to make sure you know the material before an exam.

Also break the material into small chunks. Scientists at the Massachusetts Institute of Technology say your brain can handle only about four pieces of information at once. Trying to study for three tests and two quizzes at the same time isn't going to work. Read a little bit on one subject, and test yourself to make sure you've got it. Take a five-minute break, and then move on to the next subject.

Study in a way that works for you. If you're most alert in the morning, study before you go to school. If you're a visual learner, draw pictures or make flash cards. If you learn best by listening, record your notes and listen to them on your MP3 player while you walk to school.

Make memorization easier with mnemonic devices. For example, use rhymes like "I before E except after C," or acronyms like HOMES (the Great Lakes: Huron, Ontario, Michigan, Erie, and Superior). Or, use visualization techniques. Imagine yourself walking through your kitchen and finding a different math

CRAMMING: WHY IT WON'T WORK

It's a Tuesday night. The big biology test is tomorrow morning. The notes are still sitting in your notebook, untouched and unread since you wrote them. You've got to cram two months' worth of schoolwork into the two hours that are left before you go to bed—or work through the night and skip sleep. You're overwhelmed, overworked, overtired, and stressed out.

Cramming isn't productive. It doesn't work. Trying to absorb large amounts of information in a short period of time is like trying to catch flies in a fishing net. You may grab one or two flies, but for each new one you catch, many more will fall out of the net. Likewise, you may shove a few facts into your brain while cramming, but most of them will slip away when the test paper is sitting in front of you. Most studies about test-taking strategies show that people remember facts and concepts better when they study them over a period of time, not one day or a couple of hours.

Don't cram. Learn the material a little bit at a time. Study for a few minutes every night. Back up and go over the parts you've already learned at the start of each study session. Then move forward to study the new material. By test time, you'll find that you're an expert on the subject and the test will be a breeze!

formula or past president in each drawer. During the test, mentally open drawers to retrieve the answers.

When you're done studying, pretend you're the teacher. "Teach" the material to your parent, sibling, or friend. If they get it, then you've got it.

The Night Before the Test

By the night before the test, you should already know the information. Now all you have to do is review it. Take out your notes and test yourself on the material, covering the answers with your hand so you can't cheat. Once you've got one section of your notes down, move on to the next section.

Start studying as soon as possible after you get home from school. Stop studying an hour or so before bedtime to give your mind a chance to absorb the material and rest.

Never pull an all-nighter before taking a test. Go to bed early so your brain will be refreshed by test time.

As for rest, go to bed early on the night before a test. Students who stay up too late have more trouble learning and paying attention in school, researchers reported in a 2005 issue of the journal *Sleep*. Middle school students need about nine hours of sleep or more each night, according to the National Sleep Foundation.

MYTHS and Facts

MYTH Tests are used to find out how much you know.

Fact This isn't quite true. No single test could measure the huge volume of knowledge inside your head. Tests check only what you know about one specific subject—such as how to multiply negative numbers or the causes of the French Revolution.

MYTH Smart people do better on tests.

Fact Anyone who listens in class, takes detailed notes, and studies hard can do well on tests.

MYTH Test anxiety is just in your head.

Fact Test anxiety is real, and it can have actual physical symptoms. You may break out in a sweat, feel dizzy or nauseated, and be unable to concentrate. These symptoms can have a big impact on your ability to do well on the test.

CHAPTER TWO

GETTING HELP

You think studying and test taking are solo endeavors—but they're not. Acing a test is a team effort. It starts with you, of course, but along with a little help from your teachers, parents, friends, and counselors. Here are some tips on how to approach people for help, and what questions to ask them.

Help from Your Teachers

Your first stop when asking for help should be your teacher. After all, he or she taught you the material in the first place! Who knows better what will be on the test than the person who is going to be grading it? Keep in mind, though, that some tests that a teacher gives students might be standardized by the local school district or state, so he or she will not know exactly what will be asked on the test. However, a teacher will know the areas that will be covered on that test.

Before approaching your teacher, it's helpful to establish a good relationship with him or her. If you sleep through the class and then rush out the door with a "See you later!" the moment it ends, you're not starting out on the right foot. Show that you're interested and involved every single day, not just on the day before the test.

See your teacher as your ally in test taking. Do your course work and be attentive in class so you feel comfortable asking your teacher for help when you need it.

Once your teacher is on your side, make your approach. Ask questions as soon as you don't understand a concept. While your science teacher is discussing photosynthesis is the best time to ask what chlorophyll is—not five minutes before the test. Raise your hand and ask the question as you think of it, or broach the subject after school. You can also ask questions about the test and how much it counts toward your grade.

Need a little extra help? Ask if your teacher can meet with you alone, or lead a study group of your classmates after school. Or, set up a time for a one-on-one meeting to go over any topics you still need to work on.

Help from Your Parents or Family Members

Your parents or other members of your family may not be mathematicians or scientists, but they can still help you study. One of the best skills parents can offer is organization. Before you ask your parents to help you get organized, though, take a quick scan of your house. If your mother is still holding on to her paper clip collection from 1975 and the den sofa is buried under a pile of old newspapers, organization may not be your parents' strongest suit. But if your home is reasonably clean and well organized, you can assume your parents have at least some expertise in that area.

Your parents can help you become organized by doing the following:

- Juggling your weekly schedule of activities (music lessons, sports, etc.) to give you enough time for homework and studying

- Helping you organize your desk and papers
- Buying you a planner to keep track of tests and assignments
- Testing you on material you need to study

Parents can also help you with homework, but tread cautiously here. If they're still convinced that Pluto is a planet or they think string theory is something you learn in orchestra, they

BUILDING A STUDY GROUP THAT WORKS

To get your homework done or study for tests, consider starting a study group. Studying in a group can be a lot more fun than studying alone, and you can sometimes pick up ideas from your friends that you wouldn't have thought of yourself. That said, not every study group is successful. If everyone's goofing off, no one learns anything.

To pull together a study group that works, make sure everyone in the group is serious about learning. Let the goofballs form their own study group.

Each member of the study group should also be open and willing to accept other opinions. A study session in which one of your friends stubbornly insists that Abraham Lincoln was the first U.S. president is not going to accomplish much.

Plan out your study sessions. Write up a schedule that includes every topic the group needs to cover. Schedule in a couple of ten-minute breaks. Plan something fun once studying is done, like ordering pizza or watching a movie.

may not be the best resources for homework help. In that case, just ask your parents for general guidance with homework and tests—not specific help in a subject. Your parents can also help by blocking distractions—like your cell phone and computer.

Help from Your Friends

Your friends have experience in the trenches with you, studying the same topics and preparing for the same tests. So when it comes time to study, they can be valuable resources. You can learn from and bounce ideas off one another. You can also encourage one another to keep studying when you start losing interest.

You have a few options when it comes to studying with other students. You can organize a study group, pair up with a study "buddy," or ask an older student to tutor you.

Ask a few of your friends to get together after school for study sessions. Studying together can help all of you learn the material.

Help from Your Counselors

If you see your school guidance counselor only when you get into trouble, you're neglecting a valuable resource. A counselor is a mine of information about how to succeed in school. You just need to tap into that source.

Set up a time to meet with your counselor. Tell him or her about any academic issues you're having. Ask what resources are available, from books to tutors. Once you've got some ideas from your counselor, set up another appointment a few weeks later so you can go over your progress and address any areas you still need to work on.

Help from Tutors

A tutor can work with students on subjects they're struggling with. There are a lot of options when it comes to tutoring. Older students or teachers at your school may tutor to earn extra money. If your brother is really good at a subject, he may tutor you for free—or work out some kind of deal with you (like making his bed for a week in exchange for tutoring sessions). You may have a learning center in your town that's staffed with tutors who will work one-on-one with you to improve your grades. There's even online tutoring, where you can work with tutors from all over the country—and the world. Getting tutored in a subject in advance, as a preventive measure, can help you avoid playing catch-up close to the test.

How do you find a good tutor? Start by asking your guidance counselor or teacher for a recommendation. You can also do a

Some students attend special programs that are held in the community, where a tutor can offer help in preparing for tests.

search for tutors online, but have your parents check carefully to make sure the person you choose is qualified.

Help from Books and the Web

Do a search for "math help" on the Internet, and it will bring up millions of different resources—many of which are free. Just about everything covered in school is explained in detail somewhere on the Web, for example on sites such as iTunes U (http://www.apple.com/education/itunes-u/), which is accessed through your school, FunBrain.com, Mathisfun.com, the Khan Academy (http://www.khanacademy.org), HippoCampus.org, or

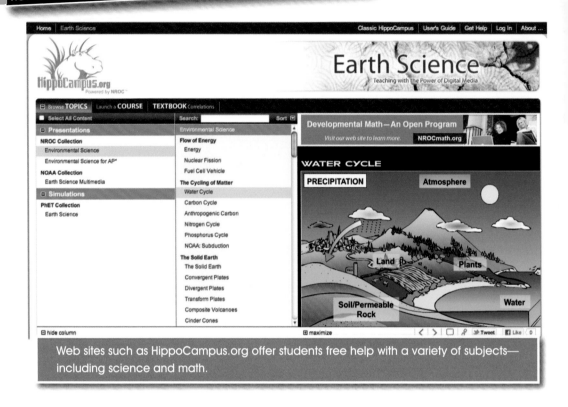

Web sites such as HippoCampus.org offer students free help with a variety of subjects—including science and math.

the American Library Association's Great Web Sites for Kids (http://www.ala.org/alsc/greatwebsites). These Web sites feature step-by-step homework and study guides on everything from calculus to the water cycle.

The best sources of information are schools, universities, and government agencies. Be wary of any sites that ask for a credit card number. Though these sites may be worthwhile resources, ask your parents before spending any money.

Books are also valuable sources of information. Go to the school or town library and ask the librarian to recommend a study guide in the subject you need. Many libraries also offer access to an online database of books, so you can browse many different study guides at once without leaving your home.

10 GreAT QUESTIONS
TO ASK A TEACHER

 1 How would you recommend I take notes for this class?

 2 How would you study if you were me?

 3 What book chapters/notes/topics will be covered on the test?

 4 Which specific parts of my notes/the book should I study?

 5 Do you have an example of an old test I can look at?

 6 Can I use my notes/textbook during the test?

 7 I spend too much time trying to figure out what questions you are really asking. Is there a method I can use that will help me understand the question so I don't overthink it and then run out of time to answer other questions?

 8 What would you suggest I do to learn more about this topic?

 9 Can you meet with me after school to go over a few things I still don't understand before the test?

 10 Can you recommend a tutor who can help me study this material?

CHAPTER THREE

DEALING WITH TEST ANXIETY

You're sitting in class, awaiting the arrival of your test paper. Even though you've studied for the test using the recommended strategies, you're a nervous wreck. How are you supposed to get an A on the test when your hands are shaking and your brain is spinning at the speed of light?

Everyone has a different response to test anxiety. Some people have real, physical symptoms. They may break out in a sweat, feel like they're about to throw up, or get so dizzy they think they're going to faint. Other people get emotional. They feel frustrated or irritable or like they're about to burst into tears.

When you feel sick, sad, or so overwhelmed that you can't concentrate on the test, anxiety is a bad thing. It's working against you and making it harder for you to succeed. Yet believe it or not, sometimes anxiety can be a good thing. It can challenge you to do your best. You can learn how to overcome test anxiety or at least make it work in your favor.

You'll be less worried and nervous on the day of the test if you review and study for it beforehand. Make sure you create a study schedule and stick to it.

What Makes You Anxious?

Every student is anxious for a different reason. Some students get distressed about taking a test because they lose confidence in themselves. They don't think they'll do well on the test. Others feel like they are stupid. Some students worry that their parents or teachers will be upset with them if they fail.

There are students who fear that this one test will mess up their whole grade for the year. Still others freeze up. They lose focus and the ability to concentrate. Or they lose their nerve because they crammed for the test the night before.

No matter what causes your anxiety, you can overcome it. Try the following strategies, and you'll be a lot calmer before your next test.

BE READY ON TEST DAY

Prepping for the test isn't just about studying. You also need to get your body and mind ready on test day. Here are a few tips:

- Go to the bathroom before the test starts. A full bladder is a big distraction.
- Get to class early.
- Sit in the front row, if possible. Then you won't be as distracted by the other students around you.
- Have all the materials you'll need—pens, pencils, calculator, and dictionary—lined up on your desk a few minutes before the test starts.
- Wear a watch so you'll know how much time is left and you can pace yourself.
- "Dump" information. Some test-taking strategists recommend doing a quick "mind dump." As soon as you get the test, write down the information that you don't want to forget—including math formulas and dates. (Other strategists, though, believe this is a technique for crammers and is not a very helpful tip.)

If you're sitting at your desk, ready to start well ahead of test time, you'll be much calmer and more collected when the test arrives.

Calm Strategy One: Become an Expert

Nothing builds confidence like knowledge. If you know exactly what to expect on the test, and you know the material inside and out, you'll have absolutely nothing to worry about on test day.

Ask your teacher questions so you'll know what topics will be covered on the test and you won't have any surprises. Review your notes and the book a few days before the exam, testing yourself over and over again until you've got the material down.

Calm Strategy Two: Relax

You can't expect to think clearly with your heart pounding and your head spinning. Take a minute or two before the test to relax your body and calm your mind with a technique called deep breathing.

First, breathe in deeply—the kind of breath your doctor asks you to take when he or she listens to your chest with a stethoscope. Hold that breath (just for a second or two—you don't want to turn blue and pass out). Now let it out slowly. Keep breathing in and out slowly and deeply for a few seconds until you feel calmer.

Another way to calm down is with progressive muscle relaxation. First tighten and then release the muscles in your feet. Now work your way up your body, tightening and releasing each group of muscles—calves, stomach, shoulders and arms, hands, face. By the time you get to your head, you should feel much more relaxed.

Calm Strategy Three: Visualize

For a minute, take yourself out of the test room. Close your eyes and picture yourself in the most spectacular scenario. You've just scored the winning touchdown at the Super Bowl. Natalie Portman is handing you an Academy Award statuette. Or your teacher has just given back your test paper with a big "100" on top.

Feel the rush of adrenaline and achievement that comes from succeeding. Now, carry that feeling of confidence back into the test room.

Calm Strategy Four:
Put It into Perspective

At least part of the anxiety you feel on test day is due to fear. You're afraid of failing the test, afraid of letting your parents down, and afraid of the impact one bad test will have on your grades. Obsessing about everything that could go wrong with the test is called "catastrophizing." It's not healthy or helpful.

Instead of catastrophizing, put your worries into perspective. Write them down on a piece of paper, and then address them, one by one. A 2011 study from the University of Chicago found that students who write down their concerns beforehand are less anxious and do better on tests.

Here's some perspective for you: what are your odds of actually failing the test? If you've studied, complete failure is probably not very likely. What will happen if you do get a lower grade than usual? Chances are it won't ruin your grade for the whole semester or year, and your teacher may even let you take the test again or make up some of the points you lost. Remember that the reality is never as terrible as you might imagine it to be.

Calm Strategy Five: Banish Negative Thoughts

When you catastrophize, all kinds of terrible thoughts race through your mind. You might think, "I'm a loser. I'm going to fail this exam." Then you picture yourself getting yelled at by your parents or flunking out of school.

Turn those negative thoughts around and replace them with positive ones such as, "I know this stuff inside and out." "I studied well, so I can pass this test." "There might be something I don't know the answer to, but I can still get a good grade." Thinking positively will give you the confidence you need to do well on the test.

Take a positive attitude with you into the test room. It's easier to succeed when you feel confident in your abilities.

Remember that no test reflects who you are as a person. When you don't do well on a test, it doesn't mean you're bad or stupid—it just means you need to work on the material a little harder.

If you're so anxious and upset about tests that you can't sleep or eat and you feel like crying all the time, talk to a doctor or counselor. What you're feeling could be part of a bigger problem called depression, and you may need to get help.

Calm Strategy Six: Prep for Test Day

You've read all the materials, asked all the questions, and studied your heart out. Now it's go time! Not so fast. You still have a couple of things to do to prep for the test, and they don't involve more studying.

A hearty breakfast of whole grains and fruit will keep you full longer so you will not have a growling stomach to distract you during the test.

Nothing is more distracting during a test than a rumbling stomach. To prevent your mind from wandering into food fantasies at test time, eat to succeed. A high-fiber, high-protein, low-sugar breakfast such as a bowl of oatmeal with fruit, or an egg-white sandwich on whole-wheat toast will keep you full for the entire test. Don't overeat, though. Eating too much at breakfast will only weigh you down and make you sleepy during the test.

Wear comfortable clothes. You should have room to move, and be dressed for the weather (a comfy sweater or sweatshirt in winter and a light T-shirt in summer). If your school has a dress code or uniform, try to wear the most comfortable clothes acceptable.

Finally, learn one more thing you need to know for the test. Reread a section of your notes that you've been struggling with. Once you've got it down, take a few minutes to relax. Read a book or listen to your favorite song to take your mind off your anxiety.

CHAPTER FOUR

HOW TO TACKLE DIFFERENT KINDS OF TESTS

Now you know how to study and how to deal with test anxiety. Next, you need to conquer the test itself. Here are a few simple tips for taking every different type of test, from multiple-choice to essays.

General Strategies for Every Test

Before getting into the specific types of tests you might take, let's cover some general test-taking strategies. These are things you should do when taking any test, whether it's an essay question about the generals of World War II or a quiz on the anatomy of an anteater.

When you get your paper on test day, have a strategy in place—a plan for how you're going to take the test. That plan could look something like the following:

1. Survey the test so you have an idea of how many questions it has.

When you get your test, quickly scan the page. See how many questions you need to answer so that you can estimate how much time you need to answer each question. You don't want to spend too much time on one question and run out of time for the others.

2. Divide the time you have available among the questions based on their point value and difficulty. Say it's an hour-long test and you have one essay question plus four short-answer questions. The essay question is worth 60 percent of the grade and it's really tough. The short-answer questions are pretty easy and count for ten points each. Budget forty minutes to work on the essay question and devote the other twenty minutes to the short-answer questions.

3. Tackle the hardest questions first. In the example above, you'd write the essay question first, then go back to answer the short-answer questions.

4. Read each question carefully, so you can answer it the right way. There's a big difference between "Fill in the definition of the highlighted word in each sentence" and "Explain why the highlighted word was used in each sentence."

5. If you're stumped on a question, move on. Come back to it later if you have time.

Looking at some specific strategies for each type of test is the next plan of action.

Multiple-Choice

It's test day. Your teacher plunks down the test paper on your desk—and it's multiple-choice. "Yes!" you think. Multiple-choice rules! All the answers are right there on the paper. You'll barely have to think! Right? Wrong. Multiple-choice tests are much harder than they look. Teachers can trick you by reordering information or presenting it in a totally different way from how you learned it. Responses that look right at first glance can be wrong.

So that you don't fall into any multiple-choice test traps, read every question carefully. Make sure you know exactly what each one is asking. Then, cover the responses and try to answer the question without looking. Lift your hand. Does any one answer on the list look close to your first guess? Then you can be pretty sure it's right.

If you're struggling with a question, here are a few tricks. Watch out for absolute words like "always" and "never." They're a clue that the answer is wrong. If two answers are opposites ("George Washington sometimes rode his horse *backward*" or "George Washington sometimes rode his horse *forward*"), there's a good chance one of them is right. By the same logic, if two choices are very similar, both of them are probably wrong. If one of the answers is "all of the above," and at least two of the responses are correct, you know that's the right response.

If you have time, save a few minutes at the end of the test so you can review your answers. Go back to the questions you had the hardest time answering and give them some more thought.

Essay Exams

For every student who loves the sight of a multiple-choice question, there's at least one who detests the sight of an essay. Essays require the most brainwork. You've got to use your mental repository of knowledge to illustrate that you not only know the information but can also analyze it and apply it in unique ways.

To prep for an essay test, review your book chapters, class notes, and homework. Look for common themes—like the role of

When answering an essay question, make sure you understand the topic well enough to analyze and explain it thoroughly and clearly.

the courts of law in the civil rights movement or how the Bill of Rights applies to everyday life. Try to ask yourself questions on the topic and answer them as clearly as you can.

Here's a tip to make these types of questions easier: look for key words that are on just about every essay test. For example:

- *Analyze*—break down the topic into its parts to explain it. The question, "Analyze the mating call of the bull-frog," is asking you to describe the sound of the mating call, what creates that sound, and how it helps the bullfrog attract a suitable mate.

- *Classify*—put things into categories. If you were asked to "Classify your friends," you might say: "John is a jock, Tim is a bookworm, and Jennifer is a fashionista."
- *Diagram*—create a drawing or chart to illustrate your answer.
- *Defend*—argue a certain position. "Defend the practice of serving chocolate bars for lunch every day" would require you to describe in detail why chocolate is healthy. In the process of defending your position, you might have to *argue* why chocolate is better than, say, peanut-butter sandwiches and *justify* its reasons for being a healthy lunch option.
- *Summarize*—write a shortened explanation of the main points. In summarizing the Magna Carta, you'd mention just the key facts about this document. "The Magna Carta is a collection of thirty-seven laws signed by King John of England in 1215, which is considered to be the beginning of constitutional government in England."

An essay test is a lot like the research papers your teacher assigns for homework. The only differences are that you've got to write it a lot faster, and you can't claim that your "dog ate your paper."

As with any research paper you write, it helps to create an outline for an essay question first so you can organize your thoughts. You can arrange your information by date (earliest to latest), by importance (most to least important), or by pros and cons. Each paragraph of your essay should cover only one topic. The first sentence of the paragraph should explain your main point. Include as much detail as possible, using examples from your books and notes to back up each point. In the last paragraph, summarize and conclude your point.

Don't throw in a lot of fluff (like a paragraph about the color of George Washington's first horse) or write in huge letters just to eat up space. Your teacher will know exactly what you're trying to pull. Alternately, don't write in tiny letters to squeeze in every single fact about George Washington, from his birth to his death. Only include the facts that are relevant to the question.

Even if spelling and handwriting don't count, try to write neatly. You can't get a good grade on a test if your teacher can't read it. Read through the essay once when you're done to make sure it's legible, and you've answered the question correctly.

Short-Answer Tests

Short-answer tests ask you to fill in a blank with a small piece of information—often a name, date, or simple fact. The best way to study for these types of tests is with flash cards.

Go through your notes and books, pulling out key terms, concepts, and dates. Test yourself over and over again until you've got these facts memorized.

Reading Comprehension

In a reading comprehension test, you have to read a few paragraphs and then answer some questions to prove how well you understood the passage. Reading comprehension questions may ask you to determine the main idea of the passage (clue: it's usually stated in the first and last paragraphs), explain the author's purpose for writing the passage, tell the difference between fact and opinion, or put events in order (clue: look for words like "first," "then," "next," and "last"). You may also have to explain which parts of the passage are more or less important, describe cause and effect (clue: look for words like "since," "because," and "as a result of"), find connections between themes, or draw conclusions.

Even if you dislike reading, you have to read the passage to answer this type of test. Skimming the paragraphs won't work. Read the whole passage, underlining important ideas or words as you go. Think about what the author is trying to say. Then for each question, reread the section of the passage to which it applies. Don't try to rely on memory alone.

Be careful when answering questions. Read all of the possible answers before responding. Remember that the answers are based on the passage, and they may not necessarily be true in real life. If a question asks, "Based on this passage, do most artists work hard?" And the passage states, "Most artists are lazy, shiftless creatures," the answer should be "no," even if your mother is an artist and she's a hard worker.

True/False

True/false tests are like multiple-choice tests, but there are only two possible answer options. The good news is that you've got a 50 percent chance of being right just by answering the question.

You should never leave anything blank on a true/false test. If you're not sure of the answer, take a guess, unless you will lose points for guessing.

Read each statement carefully, as a whole sentence. If part of the sentence is false, assume that the entire statement is false. Certain absolute words are also clues that the statement is false,

STANDARDIZED TESTS

Every year, you and your classmates get marched into the school cafeteria or a classroom and have to submit to some general test—usually of English and math. These tests are called "standardized" because most every student in your grade across the country will take the same exact test. A standardized test may not affect your grade in class, but it can tell how well you're doing in school compared to other kids your age.

Many of the same tips apply to standardized tests as to most of the tests you take in class. Eat a good breakfast, pace yourself so you don't run out of time, read the directions carefully, and answer the questions you know first. To get the hang of taking standardized tests, take a sample test, which is available in books and on several test prep Web sites. You can find a list of your state's standardized tests, along with test preparation information, on Time4Learning (http://www.time4learning.com/testprep) or sample tests on EDinformatics (http://edinformatics.com/testing/testing).

like "always," "never," "nobody," and "everyone." Qualifiers like "sometimes," "maybe," and "some" can be signs that the statement is true.

Vocabulary Tests

English teachers give vocabulary tests to see how well students have learned the words in their classroom books and notes. The best way to study for these tests is to read as much as possible. Every time you come across a word you don't understand in a book, highlight or circle it, and then look it up in the dictionary. By test time, you'll have procured a prodigious profusion of prose (that means you'll have learned a lot of words).

During the vocabulary test, read each question carefully. Look for clues to the meaning of the word in the sentence. For example, say you were given the question, "We *dissected* the frog to look at its heart, lungs, and stomach." You can guess that the word "dissected" has something to do with cutting the frog open because that's the only way you could get a glimpse of its internal organs. If you still have no clue about the word's meaning, try each of the possible answers in the sentence to see which one fits best.

Math Tests

Math tests are all about numbers—multiplying them, dividing them, using them to figure out the size and degree of angles, and combining them in different ways to solve problems. Math tests are pretty straightforward because often there's only one method and answer. Adding 12 + 12 is always going to equal

When solving problems on math tests, often you'll need to show all the steps in your solution. Showing all your work helps the teacher see how you arrived at the correct—or incorrect—answer.

24. Still, you can get into trouble if you don't read the question carefully. If the question is asking for a "sum" and you divide instead of add, your answer will be wrong.

A few days before a math test, practice all the different types of problems that will be on the test, so you'll know how to solve them. Make up a sheet of formulas to memorize. During the test, show your work (if your teacher requests it). After you're done solving a problem, check over your answer and the process you used to get there. Make sure your numbers add up (or subtract or multiply) correctly and that every decimal is in the correct place.

Now you've got some strategies to master all the different types of tests you might expect to see in class. There's still one more step to take—and it comes *after* the test.

CHAPTER FIVE

AFTER THE TEST

The teacher has collected your test, and you can finally breathe a sigh of relief. It's over! You're done with the studying and the worrying. You can relax!

Hold on there for a minute. You're not quite finished yet. The period of time after a test is the perfect opportunity for you to review the test and look for ways that you can improve on the next one.

Don't Toss Your Test—Review It!

Most students have one of two reactions when they get their graded test back. One is a feeling of elation—"Yay, I got an A!" And the other is a feeling of disappointment—"Oh brother, I got a C again!" In the former case, you may want to run home and proudly display your test on the fridge. In the latter case, you feel a strong urge to ditch the test in the nearest trash can. Don't do either. Review your test.

Check every answer against your class notes and book. See why you got answers wrong, so those same mistakes won't trip

Ask your teacher to go over your test results with you. That way, you'll be able to understand what you did wrong and avoid making the same mistakes next time.

you up on the next test. You can also double-check your teacher's grading. Teachers aren't perfect, and you might catch a mistake that could earn you back points.

Once you've gone through the test yourself, ask your teacher to review it with you. Get advice on areas where you're having trouble, so you can do better on future tests. Also ask how you did compared to your classmates and what grading criteria the teacher used. Those are valuable pieces of information you can use on the next test. Finally, save the test in a binder so you can use it when you study for your final exam.

BOUNCING BACK FROM AN F

No grade is more feared and detested than an F. Fs have earned their reputation because of the impact they have not just on your grade but also on your self-esteem. They should be seen as a starting point for improvement. Try to raise your grade by working with your teacher, studying harder, and getting help from a peer or tutor. Determine what mistakes you made, and try not to make the same mistakes on the next test. See if you can figure out what your weak points are and improve on them. Practice true/false questions if those are your downfall. Try to study in an environment that is free from distractions. If you can do extra credit or take the test again to bring up your grade, go for it! Most important, don't get discouraged. Your grade doesn't define you. It's just one little blip in what will otherwise be a very successful school career.

Common Test Mistakes and How to Avoid Them

Sometimes you can attribute a poor grade to a lack of studying. But there are certain stupid mistakes people make on tests that also steal points from their grade. Here are a few of these mistakes and some ways to avoid them:

Mistake: You misread the question. It asked for the part of speech and you gave the definition instead.
Solution: Read questions completely and slowly so you know exactly what they're asking.

Mistake: You copied the answer wrong from your piece of scratch paper. Instead of writing "24" as your answer to "What is 12 x 2," you wrote "42."
Solution: Check over your work carefully, looking for spelling, grammatical, and numerical mistakes before you turn it in so you don't make careless errors.

Mistake: You left out an important detail in the answer.
Solution: Budget your time so you won't be rushed. Leave enough time to answer every question and review your answers.

Carefully budgeting your time during the test can help avoid all three of these mistakes. By leaving enough time at the end of the test, you'll be able to review your work and make sure it's correct.

Anyone who studies hard and puts in enough effort in learning the material can receive an A on a test. Achieving a perfect score is an honor and recognizes a student's excellent performance.

Moving Forward to the Next Test

The test is finished. You've gotten your grade, reviewed it, and now you're ready to move on. Hopefully, you now have some helpful strategies to make test taking a less painful process in the future.

Now that you know how to study for tests, avoid the choking anxiety, and bounce back from a low grade, the only step you have left to do is to move forward. Approach the next test with a feeling of hopeful excitement, not dread. Know that you are smart enough and talented enough to get an A not just once but on every single test you take.

glossary

abbreviation A shortened version of a word. An abbreviation for United States is U.S.

acronym A word that is formed by putting together the first letters of a sentence or phrase. ASAP is an acronym for the phrase "as soon as possible."

analyze To explain a subject by breaking it up into its different parts.

catastrophize To make a situation seem much worse than it really is.

chunking The practice of breaking large study sessions into smaller "chunks" of time.

classify To arrange something by category. For example, in an animal classification system, dogs are classified as mammals.

criticize To judge yourself or someone else, or speak harshly about the person.

depression A feeling of sadness that lasts for several weeks.

intimidated Feeling fearful of a person because of his or her power or wealth.

invoke To declare that something is in effect, such as a law or right.

justify To show or prove why something is right.

legible Writing that is clear enough to be read.

loathing An intense hatred or dislike of something or someone.

mnemonic A device used to help you remember. HOMES is a mnemonic device for the Great Lakes—Huron, Ontario, Michigan, Erie, and Superior.

patented The protection of an invention or process, which gives its owner the right to use or sell it exclusively for a certain number of years.

progressive muscle relaxation A technique in which a person tenses and then releases the muscles of his or her body to promote a state of relaxation.

regurgitate To repeat back information without understanding it.

repository A place where information or other things can be stored.

standardized test A test that asks all students throughout an area or country the same questions.

visualization A technique in which your mind goes to a different place to help you relax or remember information.

American School Counselor Association (ASCA)
1101 King Street, Suite 625
Alexandria, VA 22314
(703) 683-ASCA
Web site: http://www.schoolcounselor.org
The ASCA promotes effective, professional, and ethical techniques for school guidance counselors in giving students
helpful assistance in all aspects of their studies, including
test-taking strategies.

Association for Middle Level Education (AMLE)
4151 Executive Parkway, Suite 300
Westerville, OH 43081
(800) 528-6672
Web site: http://www.amle.org
AMLE is a group of principals, teachers, parents, and other people
who are responsible for educating middle school students.

Canadian Education Association (CEA)
119 Spadina Avenue, Suite 705
Toronto, ON M5V 2L1
Canada
(416) 591-6300
Web site: http://www.cea-ace.ca
The CEA is the Canadian organization that works with teachers
and school leaders to help students succeed.

Canadian School Boards Association (CSBA)
1410 Rue Stanley, Bureau 515
Montreal, QC H3A 1P8
Canada
(514) 289-2988
Web site: http://cdnsba.org
CSBA members represent school boards throughout Canada.
They serve more than three million elementary, middle, and
high school students across the country.

Educational Testing Service (ETS)
Rosedale Road
Princeton, NJ 08541
(609) 921-9000
Web site: http://www.ets.org
ETS develops, administers, and scores more than fifty million
tests every year. Its Web site provides information for test
preparation.

National Education Association (NEA)
1201 Sixteenth Street NW
Washington, DC 20036-3290
(202) 833-4000
Web site: http://www.nea.org
The NEA has been around since 1857. Its goal is to provide a
quality education for every student in America.

National Tutoring Association (NTA)
P.O. Box 6840
Lakeland, FL 33807-6840
(863) 529-5206
Web site: http://www.ntatutor.com
The NTA is the largest organization of tutors. It represents
   tutors in the United States and thirteen other countries.

Web Sites

Due to the changing nature of Internet links, Rosen Publishing
has developed an online list of Web sites related to the subject
of this book. This site is updated regularly. Please use this link
to access the list:

http://www.rosenlinks.com/MSSH/Tests

Barnekow, Daniel. *3-D Graphic Organizers: 20 Innovative, Easy-to-Make Learning Tools That Reinforce Key Concepts and Motivate All Students!* New York, NY: Scholastic, 2009.

Brown, Lauren. *Girls' Life Ultimate Guide to Surviving Middle School.* New York, NY: Scholastic, 2010.

Cassel, Katrina L. *The Middle School Survival Manual.* St. Louis, MO: Concordia College, 2010.

DK Publishing. *How to Be a Genius.* London, England: DK Publishing, 2009.

Galbraith, Judy. *The Gifted Teen Survival Guide: Smart, Sharp, and Ready for (Almost) Anything.* Minneapolis, MN: Free Spirit Publishing, 2011.

Hippie, Deana. *Note Taking Made Easy! Strategies & Scaffolded Lessons for Helping All Students Take Effective Notes, Summarize & Learn the Content They Need to Know.* New York, NY: Scholastic, 2010.

McKellar, Danica. *Math Doesn't Suck: How to Survive Middle School Math Without Losing Your Mind or Breaking a Nail.* New York, NY: Penguin Group, 2008.

Munroe, Erin A. *The Anxiety Workbook for Girls.* Minneapolis, MN: Fairview Press, 2010.

Nalk, Anita. *Beat Stress! The Exam Handbook.* New York, NY: Crabtree Publishing Company, 2009.

Phipps, Tessa. *Study for Success.* Chicago, IL: Heinemann Raintree, 2008.

Rozakis, Laurie. *Get Test Smart! The Ultimate Guide to Middle School Standardized Tests.* New York, NY: Scholastic, 2007.

Sirotowitz, Sandi. *Study Strategies Plus: Building Study Skills and Executive Functioning for School Success.* Plantation, FL: Specialty Press/A.D.D. Warehouse, 2012.

Sorsa, A. T. *Time Management for Girls: A Quick Help Book.* Charleston, SC: CreateSpace, 2012.

Stern, Judith M., and Uzi Ben-Ami. *Many Ways to Learn: A Kid's Guide to LD.* Washington, DC: Magination Press, 2010.

Warner-Prokos, LuAnn, and Tami Pleasanton. *Study Skills Tool Kit Revised Edition.* Deerfield Beach, FL: Palm Tree Educational Press, 2008.

Brigham Young University. "Test Taking Strategies." Retrieved December 15, 2011 (http://ccc.byu.edu/casc/test-taking-strategies).

Davis, Bertha. *How to Take a Test.* New York, NY: Franklin Watts, 1984.

Fallone, Gahan, Christine Acebo, Ronald Seifer, and Mary A. Carskadon. "Experimental Restriction of Sleep Opportunity in Children: Effects on Teacher Ratings." *Sleep*, Vol. 28, No. 12, December 2005, pp. 1,561–1,567.

Finn, Emily. "When Four Is Not Four, But Rather Two Plus Two." MIT.edu, June 23, 2011. Retrieved December 19, 2011 (http://web.mit.edu/newsoffice/2011/miller-memory-0623.html).

Gettysburg Foundation. "Battle of Gettysburg." Retrieved January 12, 2012 (http://www.gettysburgfoundation.org/37/battle-of-gettysburg).

GreatSchools Staff. "Free Tutoring Under the No Child Left Behind Law." GreatSchools.org. Retrieved February 9, 2012 (http://www.greatschools.org/students/homework-help/123-free-tutoring-no-child-left-behind.gs).

GreatSchools Staff. "Study and Test-taking Strategies for Kids with Learning Difficulties." GreatSchools.org. Retrieved December 15, 2011 (http://www.greatschools.org/students/academic-skills/627-study-and-test-taking-strategies-for-kids-with-learning-difficulties.gs).

GreatSchools Staff. "Study Skills for Middle School and Beyond." GreatSchools.org. Retrieved December 15, 2011 (http://www.greatschools.org/students/homework-help/322-study-skills-for-middle-school-and-beyond.gs).

GreatSchools Staff. "Thinking of Getting a Tutor? Ten Questions You Must Ask." GreatSchools.org. Retrieved February 9, 2012 (http://www.greatschools.org/students/homework-help/122-finding-a-tutor-questions-to-ask.gs).

Greenberg, Michael. *Painless Study Techniques*. Hauppauge, NY: Barron's Educational Services, Inc., 2009.

Harms, William. "Writing About Worries Eases Anxiety and Improves Test Performance." UChicago.edu, January 13, 2011. Retrieved February 15, 2012 (http://news.uchicago.edu/article/2011/01/13/writing-about-worries-eases-anxiety-and-improves-test-performance).

Muskingum College. "Test Taking Strategies." Retrieved December 15, 2011 (http://www.muskingum.edu/%7Ecal/database/general/testtaking.html).

National Parks Service. "Battle Summary: Chickamauga, GA." Retrieved January 12, 2012 (http://www.nps.gov/hps/abpp/battles/ga004.htm).

National Sleep Foundation. "How Much Sleep Do We Really Need?" Retrieved January 12, 2012 (http://www.sleepfoundation.org/article/how-sleep-works/how-much-sleep-do-we-really-need).

Nemours Foundation. "Studying for Tests." November 2008. Retrieved December 15, 2011 (http://kidshealth.org/teen/school_jobs/school/test_terror.html).

Piscitelli, Steve. *Study Skills: Do I Really Need This Stuff?* Upper Saddle River, NJ: Prentice Hall, 2008.

Scholastic. "Test-Taking Strategies for Three Subject Areas." Scholastic.com. Retrieved December 15, 2011 (http://www.scholastic.com/teachers/article/test-taking-strategies-three-subject-areas).

Shellenbarger, Sue. "Toughest Exam Question: What Is the Best Way to Study?" *Wall Street Journal*, October 26, 2011. Retrieved December 15, 2011 (http://online.wsj.com/article/SB10001424052970204644504576653004073453880.html#0).

University of Guelph Library. "Multiple Choice Exams." Retrieved December 15, 2011 (http://www.lib.uoguelph.ca/assistance/learning_services/handouts/multiple_choice_exams.cfm).

York University. "Preparing for Tests and Exams." February 25, 2008. Retrieved December 15, 2011 (http://www.yorku.ca/cdc/lsp/skillbuilding/exams.html#Working).

index

About the Author

Stephanie Watson is an award-winning writer based in Atlanta, Georgia. She is a regular contributor to several online and print publications, and she has written or contributed to more than twenty-four books.

Photo Credits

Cover © iStockphoto.com/Christopher Futcher; pp. 3, 4–5 © iStockphoto.com/Jose Gil; pp. 5, 31 Fuse/Thinkstock; p. 9 Konstantin Chagin/Shutterstock.com; p. 11 Trish Gant/Dorling Kindersley/Getty Images; p. 13 jcjgphotography/Shutterstock.com; p. 15 Hemera/Thinkstock; p. 18 Lorraine Swanson/Shutterstock.com; p. 21 KidStock/Blend Images/Getty Images; p. 23 Steve Smith/Digital Vision/Getty Images; p. 24 © Copyright 2012 Monterey Institute for Technology and Education, all rights reserved; p. 27 Jupiterimages/Comstock/Thinkstock; p. 32 msheldrake/Shutterstock.com; p. 35 Fuse/Getty Images; p. 38 Jupiterimages/Goodshoot/Thinkstock; p. 44 iStockphoto/Thinkstock; p. 47 Jack Hollingsworth/Photodisc/Thinkstock; p. 50 Jupiterimages/Photos.com/Thinkstock; cover and interior graphics (arrows) © iStockphoto.com/alekup.

Designer: Nicole Russo; Editor: Kathy Kuhtz Campbell; Photo Researcher: Karen Huang